BY

ELIZABETH KNIGHTLY

1st Edition | 01
Hardcover ISBN: 979-8-9890939-0-8

First Published October 2023

Also Available in Paperback:
979-8-9880379-7-2

For inquiries and bulk orders, please email:
indieearthbooks@gmail.com

Printed in the United States of America   1 2 3 4 5 6 7 8 9

Indie Earth Publishing Inc.
| Miami, FL |

www.indieearthbooks.com

INDIE EARTH
PUBLISHING

Praise for *Choose To Choose Me*

"Elizabeth Knightly's *Choose To Choose Me* not only showcases beautiful poetry but unveils a deep unspoken honesty of self. These poems are letters of love, not only to the ones who got away, but to Knightly herself. *Choose To Choose Me* is a poetry collection I will be frequently revisiting." — John Queor, Author of *Bypass*

"Elizabeth Knightly goes the extra mile to immerse you in her world. With song recommendations accompanying each poem, Knightly provides a musical backdrop that allows her readers to experience the emotions as vividly as she did with her Muses. The pain of judgment and dismissal is juxtaposed with the warmth and acceptance found in the arms of a kindred spirit. *Choose To Choose Me* is a tale of transformation, exploring the complexities of love, passion, and personal growth." — Catalina Prieto, Author of *transcend*

"*Choose To Choose Me* is an invigorating journey unraveling the female experience, as well as our relationships with others, and most importantly, ourselves. Like choosing the perfect glass of wine to sip with your favorite meal, Knightly has hand picked songs to pair with each poem. Swifties will rejoice in all of the "Taylor-coded" references, but anyone can be moved by the visceral imagery and vulnerability woven into these pages." — Marlina Mossberg, Author of *Peach*

"With *Choose to Choose Me*, Elizabeth Knightly crafts a songbook of poetry, relying on simplicity and clarity of language to slowly build rhythms, making her verses universal ear-worms that stay with you long after you put down this book. She normalizes concepts like eroticism, nostalgia, and magical realism in a distinct rejection of the male gaze, turning it against itself to seek accountability for the commodification of women and the price that is paid in sexuality, feelings of self-worth, romantic disillusionment, body dysmorphia, depression, and eating disorders, among other things. Through this journey, the reader will witness the triumphant assertion that, even as one traverses through adversity, choosing yourself is the best choice you will ever make; that you are and have always been more than enough." — Renzo Del Castillo, Author of *Still*

"Elizabeth Knightly's debut poetry collection, *Choose To Choose Me*, is a wonder. Through her powerful words and carefully curated accompanying songs, Knightly invites the reader on a journey alongside herself and her Muses. Together, you traverse the waters of inspiration, heartbreak, and self-discovery. This collection will leave you thinking long after you leave its pages and forever changed for the better." — Azure Hall, Author of *Reflections: A Mythology in Poetry & Prose*

"*Choose To Choose Me* is a lovely little collection. As a fellow Swiftie, I really enjoyed all the references, and the passion and rawness is so strong and powerful throughout the entire book. Knightly writes so vividly and her word choice is expressed so beautifully. I look forward to reading more from this author!" — Alexandra J. Vincent, Author of *Sugar Too Sweet*

"Elizabeth Knightly's debut poetry collection *Choose To Choose Me* is a soundtrack in poetry to finding love, losing it, realizing its all messy anyway, and then finding yourself. It's lyrical, relatable, and downright meaningful with all the little pieces of herself Knightly puts in. It's cakey in the best way possible and a beautiful homage to the journey one goes through and grows through in learning to always choose yourself." — Flor Ana, Author of *The Truth About Love*

"*Choose to Choose Me* is a sweet melodic look at a Swiftie's sometimes struggle and love life. It's about finding self-acceptance, and I really identified with Knightly's candid poems on body image challenges. It's the kind of book my 20-year-old self desperately needed long ago." — Annie Vazquez, Author of *My Little Prayer Book: 75 Prayers, Poems and Mantras for Illumination*

Choose To Choose Me:

A Collection of Organized Chaos

Elizabeth Knightly

"To the ones I've loved, the ones I've hated,
the ones I've fucked and sometimes dated."
-*Unknown*

Dear Reader,

4 muses, 5 chapters, 45 poems. A combination of the energies in angel number 4 and angel number 5. A message of passion, harmony, adventure, and growth—from my angels to you. It was not my intention, but as this project unfolded, the 'Swiftie' in my subconscious took over and decided to make this very personal piece of my heart "Taylor-coded" *(which, honestly, is my heart's most authentic form of expression.)*

Thank you for picking this up, taking the time to read it, and holding space for my words. I have always been the type of person whose words seemingly fail me in conversation, but seamlessly pour out of me on paper. I found that I best express myself to people by making playlists for them, so that's exactly what I did here, for you. *Choose To Choose Me* isn't a linear experience with a set ending. Instead, it is a cyclical connection where we are consistently choosing each other.

So, to truly transport you into every freeze-frame moment I've captured in each poem, I am adding song recommendations *(they won't all be Taylor)*. The lyrics, the energy of the music, and sometimes even the lore tied to a song will allow you to live exactly what I felt with my muses or when reflecting and writing about them.

Thank you for *choosing* me.

- Elizabeth Knightly

Background

Let's relive it together, through muses. The table of contents will use the title of Taylor Swift songs to introduce you to each of my muses. The songs, faithful reader, will be a debriefing—what it feels like to love and know each muse. Ready to travel back in time with me?

Two muses:
Gold Rush and **Daylight**
Brilliant,
Brave,
Bold.
Each left their mark
On my soul.
Whether they know it
Or not.
When there is a poem
Inspired by <u>both of them</u>,
Find it in
The Archer.

One muse
Is complex with facets
Faces, and pages.
A **Mirrorball**,
Illuminating scraps
On how she sees the world;
Shards of trauma
And healing
Elaborately embedded
In each other.

The final muse
Is *only* to conclude
All metaphorical chapters.
Everyone, here and accounted for,
A curtain close.
I Forgot That You Existed;
I never imagined I'd care so little
About a 5-year phase.

Choose To Choose Me

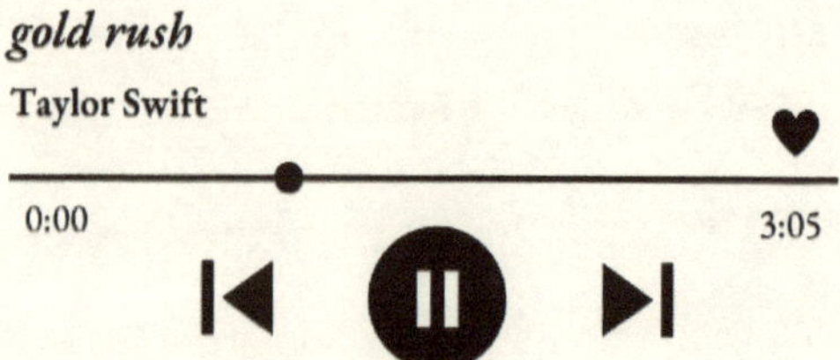
gold rush
Taylor Swift
0:00
3:05

I'm Kissing You
Des'ree
0:29
4:53

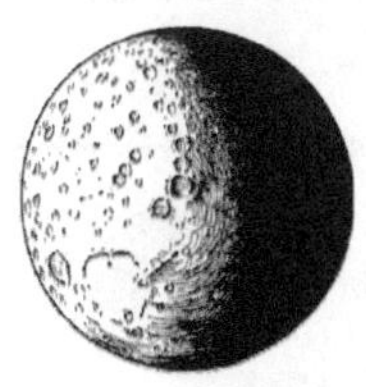

To my *Gold Rush**

To get to know this muse play *gold rush* by Taylor Swift

*Do you remember what I said about our kiss on the church steps? *I'm Kissing You* by Des'ree; start at the time stamp 2:55 *(let it play till the end)*. That is exactly what I was trying to put into words. I'm happy I can finally share half of what I felt that night with you. Every time I listen to it, it's an all-consuming experience, feelings rush and flood. I get to relive that moment, and for a couple of seconds, it almost feels like our love is alive and thriving again.

Better Man (Taylor's Version) (From The Vault)
Taylor Swift
1:36
2:13

Double Minded

Blushing rosebuds paint his lips
Reflections of iridescent satin create his sighs
Soft yet bright,
Tenderness and seduction dress his boyish eyes
With summer in his heart,
Warm amber glows in his soul
Each kiss more decadent than the last,
Every illustrious riches' lustre
With a taste of heaven,
His supple skin is more than a celestial cloth
Sultry man,
I adore you
Combative man,
I abhor you

Be More

Stephen Sanchez

1:11   3:51

Wrong Turn in Eden (Part I)

You fear for your freedom
I fear for my capture
Right person, wrong time
What if this is the rapture?
Contentions, contingencies
All it allows is fear to breed
When we kiss,
My first real breath I breathe
I've always been dormant. Asleep...
Didn't realize I wasn't awake until our first meet

We sit beneath a blood moon
And in my head I release
I ask the sanctity of the stars
Take power and make what's ours
Come true

I've told the moon about you,
Before
Now, here, she sees you, sitting beside me, below her
Be more...
Remove all the obstacles,
All the dread,
All the human that gets in one's head
Release the torture and the trepidation,
Release thoughts of complications;
Let us be free of our heads so this pursuit can thrive and drive
Let us dive into a marital bed
What of nonsense?
What of sense?
It is only human to overlook and overcomplicate what heaven sent
Mistrusting, rationalizing...

Bedroom Hymns
Florence + The Machine
0:28
3:01

Wrong Turn in Eden (Part II)

I know your God might not be mine
And the future of teachings and preachings hang nether by,
But what if we just ride?
What if we are meant?
What if we were created
Like Adam, like Eve?
Purposefully crafted, destined to meet,
But this time, we complete the feat
You and I are meant to combine
Like two unlikely colors,
Making the most gorgeous painted blend
What if we are one?
United
What if we are
The one?
To end all fights?
...I think you know it
You feel it too...
I think you're scared we're the sacred two

Dirty Thoughts

Chloe Adams

0:00   2:09

Bare Hands

Monet's brushstrokes do not compare;
Lace embraces from his fingertip caresses
The artistic balance of heavy breath
Strokes replicating primal harmonies that echo,
Pulsate and drum. Hallowed doors sprawl;
Exchanges of flesh crawl, bested and blest
Maroon-mist envelopes, staining pearl
Sheets velvet with our essence
Your presence, effervescent
Secreting consecrated potions
Lovers blossom and protest
Loins far too unruly to rest
Worships his artistry, this bosom
This masterpiece
You make me feel...
A whole woman

Not How I Want To
Zach Seabaugh
0:00
2:54

Dew Drops on Crimson Leaves

Star crossed skies,
Green-eyed with envy,
Their unity a legendary entity

He mended her meaning of comfort;
She ensured that he never again
Felt anything remotely close to nothing

Walking in intuition,
Both melting into the uncensored experience,
For a brief moment in time
Two destined souls conquered redamancy

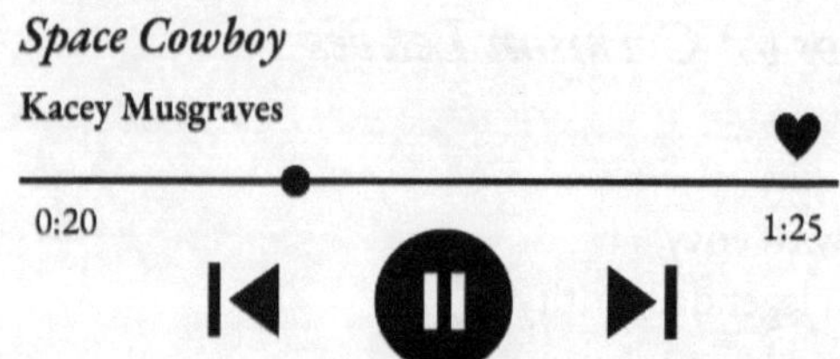

Space Cowboy
Kacey Musgraves
0:20
1:25

Ramblin' Man (Part I)

So you wanna be a cowboy?
Giddy up, ride away
You wanna be a ramblin' man?
'Cause you don't know how to stay
You'll always hide,
Always run away
From your own secrets and trials;
You live in denial
Hold back what you wanna say;
Slave to your old ways
Shackled by the waves
Of concrete burdensome restraint
You'll never know how to say
What you want to communicate
Operating in survival,
Your life forever on trial
Terrified to stray
Too far away,
The restless oceans relay
As we fade in your disarray
Take flight,
Rushing, running
Never interested in catching
Your breath
Don't you grow tired
When it gets quiet?
The darkness concaves
Don't you long for an old new day?
Always the stranger,
Always never not in danger
So you wanna be a cowboy?
Giddy up, run away

I Wish you Roses

Kali Uchis

1:01   1:35

Ramblin' Man (Part II)

You wanna be a ramblin' man
I guess your punishment is ramblin' you'll stay
As the days pass away
Your impertinence toward rest will lay
Waste your life,
Years and days

Something in the Orange

Zach Bryan

0:00   2:28

Elle

As the River Flows

Some things are better left unsaid

I don't want to know what's in your head
I don't want to know the fears you dread,
The tears you tread

All that work to crack me open
Now, I'm obsessed
All that work, while you're repressed

Speaking to me whole,
You left me for dead
Sitting in your mind,
On cold cement
Holding onto our last breaths

You say that you love me... Well, you guess
Now,
We're both left broken and undressed
Gambling with my heart,
You racked up debt

I'd like to say I hate you, but I have no regrets;
Giving me your demons whilst I wept
You wipe my tears away as sunset sets

Barely hanging on by orange thread,
There's something in this love...
Too much depth

Some things are better left unsaid

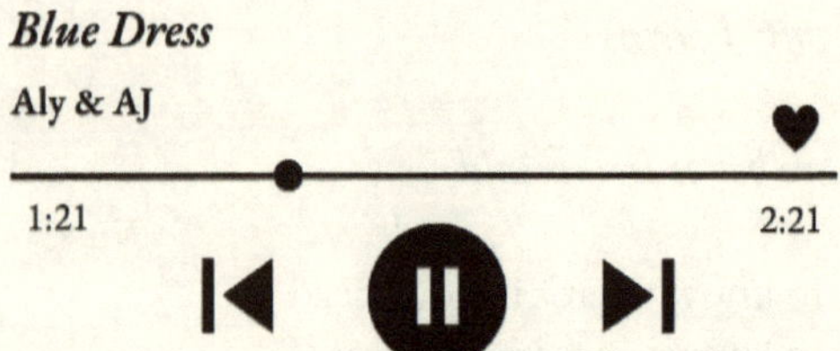

Blue Dress
Aly & AJ
1:21
2:21

Stolen Street Signs

Wood rot
Plagued our love
The ghost of you
Terrorizes the streets
Where the fireworks
Began, when you took my hand
Enchanted to meet you,
Had my whole family greet you
From October to December
I still remember,
In the blink of an eye,
You made me kiss it all goodbye
Like sea salt and thyme,
The river
When you were mine
Under the crystal clear
Full moon sky,
You'd always call at midnight
We slow-danced to sweet nothings
Like a picture to burn
Ingrained in my mind
Now every vintage truck
Turns into a meaningless one night fuck
As I'm searching for you
In each and every thrust
Any piece I can get
To bring me closer
To what your heartbeat used to feel like on my chest
Memories of you,
Was it all a ruse?
'Cause I can't keep up
With what was true in what you rued
Wrote some songs about you,
But I'm still
Paralyzed, lifeless,
Unhinged, unglued,
At the potential sight of you

Playing God
Paramore
1:09
1:36

Sailor of Solitude

Cold shoulder,
Cruel soldier,
What's it like getting older?
How's it feel never being sober?

Blow out your candles,
No one's there to celebrate
You're chasing heathens
'Cause your demons ain't celibate

You're preaching heaven,
But you're crippled by shame
As you ordain your ways
Casting shadows away

Chasing bottles all day,
Just to live with the pain
Of the souls you still take

Your own spirit,
Your own heart
You like to break

Come correct wayward saint

The River
Daisy Jones & The Six
1:26
3:00

Dear Soldier

You left me
Stranded
Doe-eyed and branded
All alone by the Mississippi,
Drowning
Consumed by you,
Your mercurial bliss
Hope you find serenity
Because it cost me
My everything

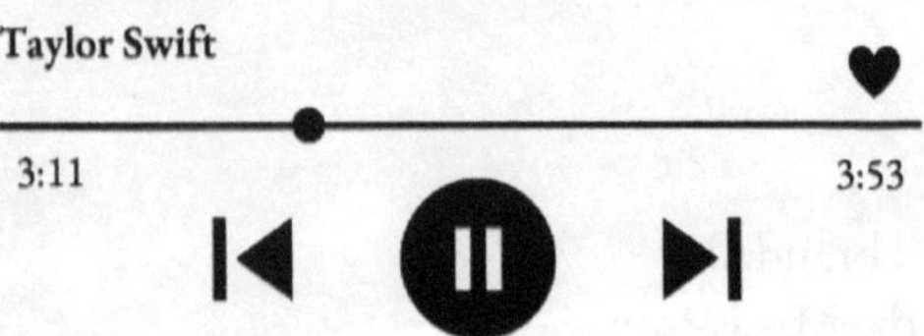

Haunted (Taylor's Version)
Taylor Swift
3:11
3:53

Man in the Arena

Bare,
Barren
Forgive myself for overstaying,
Waiting too long
Oversharing was wrong
We simply don't belong
Now that we're done,
Now that you're gone,
How are you so strong?

Colder Weather

Zac Brown Band

1:42   4:33

Preference for Suffering

You're in my arms,
No composure,
No closure

Lonely boy
The woods could never tame
Shred me to pieces while your verses are insane
You're quick to judge but never hold blame
In your wretched game
That you've come to play
What could you ever gain?

No one's there to hold your pain,
Casting any semblance of resemblance away
All by my name
As you weep between my thighs
My love was his sacred cry
We tried to save you, him and I
While the devil ate you alive

Look in the mirror
Only you can break the chains
Only you, can't self-sustain
Lonely boy who pushes away
Lonely boy
The woods could never tame

Nothing Compares 2 U

Sinéad O'Connor

0:00

4:40

Shattered Moonstone

Everybody wants a piece of me,
But nobody really cares
My therapist is fed up with me
Says I'd rather give my body
Than a soulful stare

I think it's a fair trade
Trying to keep my sanity;
How can I commit to you
Knowing all you do is leave?

Everybody wants a piece of me,
But nobody really cares
I kiss all the boys,
I let them feel me,
But I swear they don't compare

You used to firestorm my bones
With your words alone
Please tell me why you're not here?
My flesh,
It's wailing your moans
You worked through all my haunted shit,
Slayed my demons and my fears

You thought I was all patched up,
Taking off on your high horse,
Leaving shreds of shattered little fragments
Where you used to appear

Everybody wants a piece of me,
But nobody really cares
You were the first one to ever see me,
And now you do it
Holding a rearview-mirror glare

Quietly Yours

Birdy

1:00   3:45

Nothing & Everything

Choose me
Long after
When the perfume of
Fascination and adoration
Wears off
Long after I've lost my novelty
When my time is no longer new
Or a sought after luxury
Still be smitten
Now that I am constant
Reliable and dependable
Always count on me
Without fault or notability
Choose to choose me
And I'll unknowingly,
Knowingly forever
Love thee

The Night We Met

Lord Huron

0:00   3:28

You Still Owe Me Norway (Part I)

It's been 8 months
Probably a little more than a year
By the time you read this

We spoke on the phone
About a week ago
I confessed,
There was nothing like us
You even said our chemistry remains
Unmatched.
Shit was hard *not* to miss

I went out last night,
The first time in months
Since our part,
Since my heart
Could grin and bear it.
I let him touch me

He clutched,
Gripped,
Grasped my neck when we kissed,
And all I could think
Was the moment
You pulled that same move
Under the October moon
The sax playing in the back
The sofa leather sticky with our crave

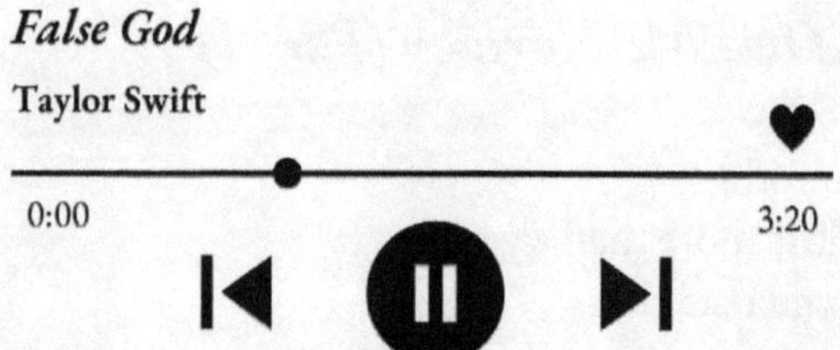

False God
Taylor Swift
0:00
3:20

You Still Owe Me Norway (Part II)

God,

I miss that,
Our fervor

I miss us
Without inhibitions,
You
The only inhabitant
Of all my submission

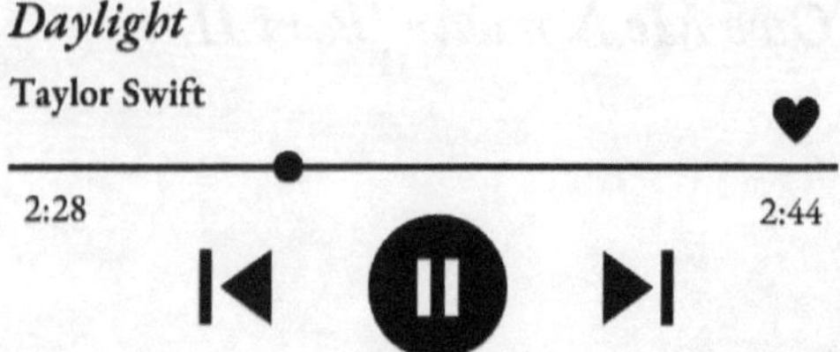

Daylight
Taylor Swift
2:28
2:44

Like A Star
Corinne Bailey Rae
0:00
0:16

To my *Daylight**

To get to know this muse play *Daylight* by Taylor Swift

*It was always about the little details with you. Everything you remembered, everything you said, crocheting cashmere sweaters to bring me back from the dead. Moments with you were always magic; the stuff of movies but never tragic. Since the first day we met, I knew you'd be special, no matter how we left. I'll make a promise to you here, now... that shooting star will forever brighten up my night skies the same way you did my mind when you were briefly mine. You are *Like A Star* by Corinne Bailey Rae.

Love Again

Dua Lipa

0:41   2:20

He Calls Me Sunshine

Your affection is an infection of attention
Establishing reflections
Of your wholesome perceptions
What I am,
Who I am in my entirety,
In this version of eternity;
I never can question your intentions
You make me feel like the exception
After a long history of
Being other men's personalized exemption
I no longer wander and wonder,
Forced to ponder my soul's reception
You have sent for me and brought back
A revival of ardent love's inception

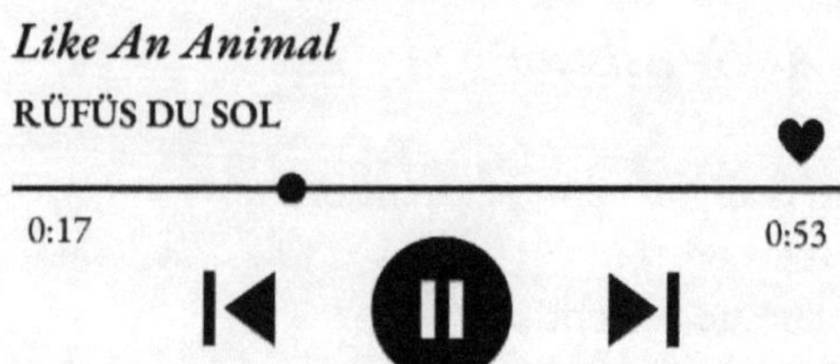

Like An Animal
RÜFÜS DU SOL
0:17
0:53

Second Chance Encounter
Previously titled 'Garnet Love'

I need a lone wolf
Yearn for a partner, not a pack
I need *follow me to the ends of the earth*
Light it up and watch it burn (together)
I need *leave it all behind*
Bonnie and Clyde
I need persistence over existence,
Courage and survival
I need intoxicating passion,
No strings to other webs
Webs entrap
Hold back
Wholly
Need devotion
Connection to one
A garnet love—
Run wild and burn the sun

Originally published in Harness Magazine

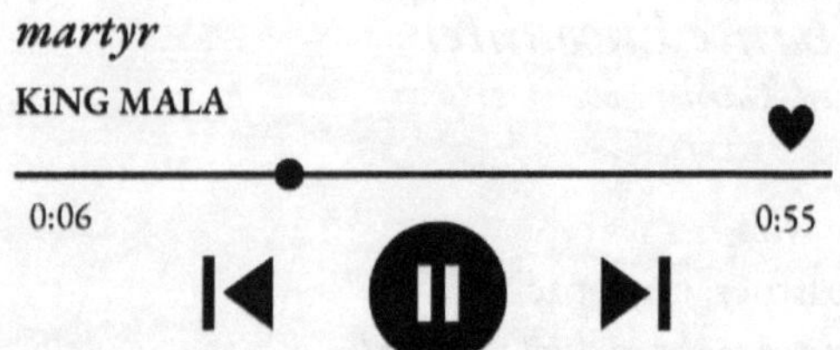

martyr
KiNG MALA
0:06
0:55

Dessert

He enters
His sacred place of worship
Pounding down on the temple doors.
Passionate in his praise, he
Bows before the sopping altar.
Sweet nectar drips from this holy ground.
Drowning him in coveted ritual,
The slippery savior of troubled men.
He sips the raw potion from a cupped breast,
To cure all his ailments.
Gulps down honeysuckle
From his favorite ripe chest.
He savors his savior's holistic way.
It's artisanal magic.
The delicacy of rites
That make men like him
Kneel before the embodiment
Of all sinfully sanctified medicine.
The ethereal drug of a delectable woman.

Snow On The Beach (feat. More Lana Del Rey)
Taylor Swift, Lana Del Rey
0:00
1:00

Confession: I Still Think About The Bridge

His ravenous hunger roared;
Her prolific compassion
Bellowed louder

Silencing his deviants.
Challenging her aspirations,
Visiting her dreams

She buried herself within
His gaping
Enigmatic thoughts

Years waned
But they remained
Living within the shade

Of one another's brain
Manifesting, envisioning, entranced
Traveling through time, hand in hand

Growing together, knowing together
Coexisting within each one's individual embodiment
Reborn into a haven for his heathens.

Cosmic health,
Sitting on the sand,
Staring at the sky

Reveling in the marvel
Of one another;
A rare infatuation.

Distracted
Russ, Bibi Bourelly
0:00
0:22

Sand and Sober Thoughts

"At least we got to check this off"
Like you could fit me into some kind of box...
I know this wasn't intense for you
It wasn't a lot

But how dare you

Have the audacity
To fold me up so neatly,
Carefully creasing my pieces,
To put me away as an afterthought?

A checklist to handle and toss;
The ghost of me, a future us,
All resolved, you absolved
It must be so nice

To shut on and shut off
Like cooled magma
And freeze dried ice.

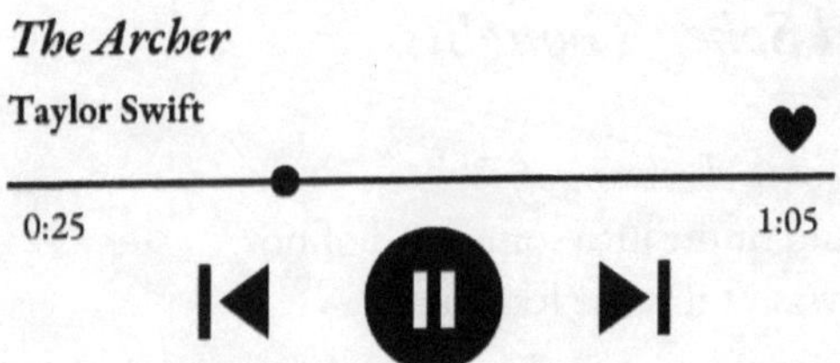

The Archer
Taylor Swift
0:25
1:05

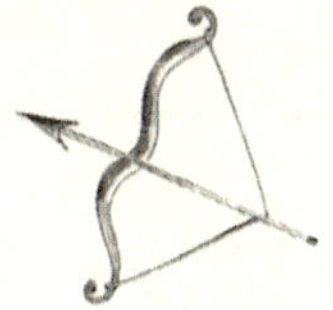

*The Archer**

To further get to know these muses play *The Archer* by Taylor Swift

*At this point, precious reader, I pray that you are well acquainted with my muses. I feel I did my best to properly and thoroughly introduce them to you. There is some kind of order to all my madness after all. And yes, the sequence of each title from previous chapters is very intentional. Now we're here, a chapter I simply had to create. It's a rare occasion when I sit down to write and find that I'm speaking to two people at once. This section addresses both muses in tandem. Hit play on *The Archer* by Taylor Swift.

I know it won't work

Gracie Abrams

1:45   2:05

The Worst Compliment

It's weird, always being the one that got
Away
Time will pass, they'll bestow it
Casually
Like it's some prize to claim
But in my head, it's more like
"The one that could never make them
Stay"

Loner
Kali Uchis
1:26
2:16

Aphrodite's Lovers - The Bridge & The River

Five second men
The irony?
They last far too long in bed
But with their hearts
Quick to depart
It's hyper-fixation,
Cerebral vacation
The lust for novelty
They drink down new personalities,
Entire persons with newfound tragedies,
Leaving them all
As common casualties
In their wake
They are men of a season,
Never with or without reason
You,
Sweet collateral
You,
Temporary adderall
Lavender haze lifted,
Pomegranate kiss jilted
The barometer of their speed
Doubles every single tear that streams

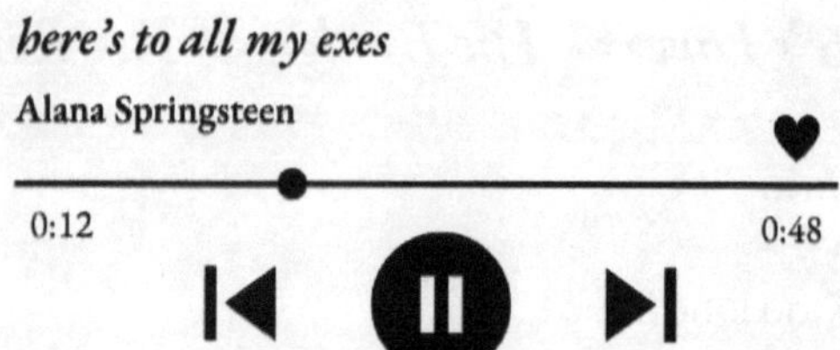

here's to all my exes
Alana Springsteen
0:12
0:48

Just so you Know

I showed him my monster

Can you believe?
He held so tight
And embraced me
Remember when I showed you?
Your cruel commentary,
Your backhanded drool
You were quick to correct,
Minimize, rebrand, redirect
You made it about you,
Left it lingering like a
Fresh cut open wound

He's tender and kind
I'm afraid to admit I get lost in his eyes
No one's better,
No one's more,
But gun to my head,
I know I'd love him more
He feels like Christmas,
Like stockings by the fireplace
He feels like home,
If there ever were a place
I'm scared I'm thinking too much,
Too far in advance,
Encapsulated by his trance
I want to get lost,
Forever wander in his chestnut glance,
Stormy sea eyes,
His honorable, humble fucking hands
I'm falling
For him;
In love
Again

I Forgot That You Existed

Taylor Swift

2:05   2:50

Should've Said No

Taylor Swift

1:51   3:39

*I Forgot That You Existed**

To get to know this muse play *I Forgot That You Existed* by Taylor Swift

*I did in fact forget this person existed until one very strange day. It felt incomplete not paying homage to what life was like before actually living. As I stated before, we're traveling back in time to when these feelings were fresh and relevant. When trying to honor this footnote in my life's pages, I could only find one poem ever written for this muse. This piece was written in the only bit of inspiration I was able to gather through half a decade. Written in the thick of feeling icky, but don't worry, *Gold Rush* made this poem quite moot the instant his eyes met mine.

Hey reader, want to know something funny? I mean, while I'm here being super transparent, I might as well, right? I had a dream where all three of these muses were at the same bar. *This* particular muse was in a dark corner and I only intuitively knew it was them. They were presented as a blurry silhouette. Meanwhile, *Daylight* and *Gold Rush* were having a battle of wits beside me while I waited for a drink. Anyway, fast forward a month—it's a Sunday, *Gold Rush* calls, *Daylight* sends a text, and me? I'm shopping for pumpkin bread ingredients at **MY** local Publix when I run into *this* muse, face to face, near the frozen chicken. We didn't exchange a word, but timing is everything... I forgot that you existed and now I am reminded so I can give this muse their final seal. So many years now seem like a blimp. I am eternally grateful that you didn't, but a younger, naiver version of myself once believed you *Should've Said No* (by Taylor Swift.)

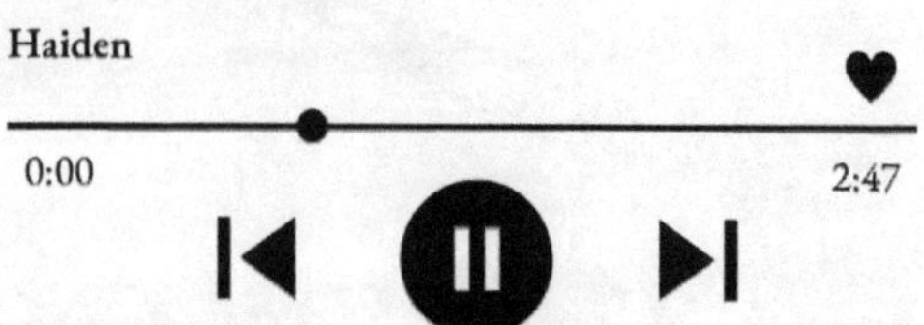

Pretty Little Addict
Haiden
0:00
2:47

Heartbreak for Christmas

I'm sitting here
Alone
It's Christmas Eve
I had to turn off my phone
You couldn't even wait till Christmas Day
To go ahead and throw my heart away
All our dreams,
All our past,
Gone up in smoke
Like lightning flash
You weren't careful;
There was too much gas
Now I don't know what to do
With all this ash.

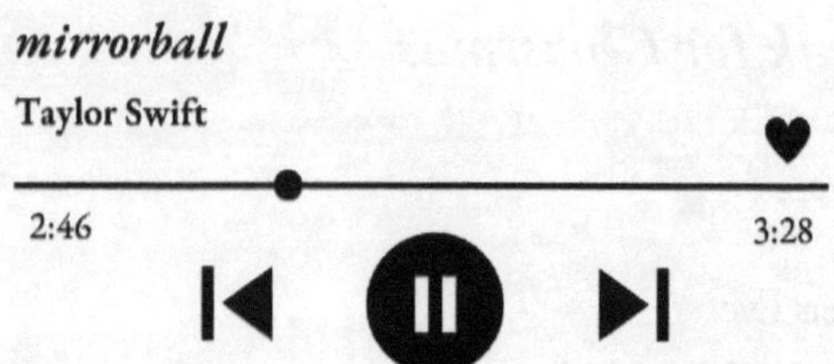

mirrorball
Taylor Swift
2:46
3:28

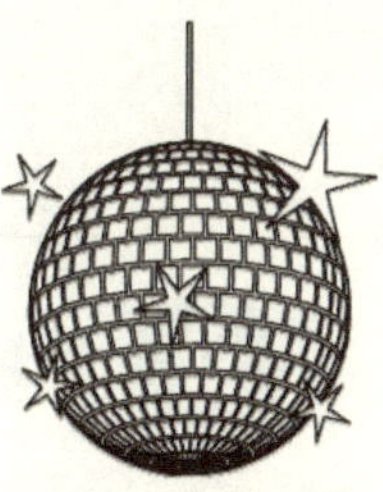

For Every *Mirrorball**

To get to know this muse play *mirrorball* by Taylor Swift

*You are not alone. I really needed that to be the first thing you read. Committed reader, you've been so good to me, so kind in *choosing* me. I don't think I could ever tangibly put into words how much you taking the time to embark into my inner workings means to me. This one is for all my *mirrorballs* out there. It's a jarring dichotomy to salute the world externally as whimsical and have your own mind be plagued by cataclysmic scenarios. This chapter is home to enchantment, inspiration and magic. But also, intrusive thoughts, rage and fury... basically, this chapter is therapy. You've journeyed through my heart and some of my soul. Now, welcome to my mind, with some of its complexities, intricacies and all of its anxieties. Turn up the volume as high as it'll let you go and dance in your room to *mirrorball* by Taylor Swift.

hypocrite
Alana Springsteen
0:10
1:54

Imposter Syndrome

Anytime,
Every time,
I attempt to get philosophical,
I consistently contemplate out loud in an accent
Does that make me a fraud, a phony? Or simply mad?
Perhaps, it's my mask.
How I must fool myself to take comfort
In my own intellect.
Too harsh to ever think
The day to day character I play,
Capable of articulating such wondrously poetic things.
Do I even deserve,
Have I earned the basic right
To speak, utterances of fond things?
Are my words even worthy
Of taking up room?
Or worse,
Being fawned over?

A Million Men

Melanie Martinez

0:22 — 4:05

Vivisteria (Part I)

I like the bits and pieces of myself
Yet to be touched by you,
Not yet quite tainted by your backwards Midas touch.

I'm still profoundly authentic, profoundly me.
You didn't get to dispirit me;
How bitter is that defeat?

**National Sexual Assault Hotline:*
800.656.4673

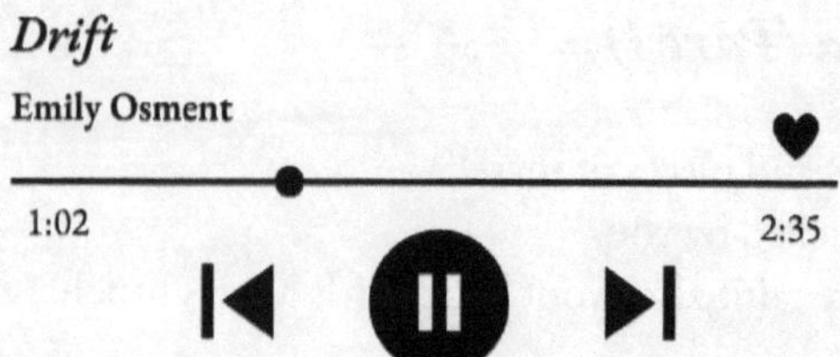

Drift
Emily Osment
1:02
2:35

Vivisteria (Part II)

Rouge of rotten roses,
Crude oil,
Powdered charcoal.

Transformation. Transmutation.
No longer milquetoast,
Even after what you stole.

The blooming bohemian within
Gave me grace and solace, again;
There is a sense of sincerity.

My earthy tones,
My sunshine bones,
Silence the treacherous tyrant winds

Whirling within me.
I sometimes still get the spins.
The wind will blow and whistle,

Hushing any fingerprint
That you may have left on me like thistle;
Quieting you,

Diminishing you,
Erasing you;
Tactics you tried to use.

**National Sexual Assault Hotline:*
800.656.4673

Skinny Love
Birdy
0:00
2:09

Holding Hands

I hate holding hands.
It's provisional permanence.
It's supposed to show
I've got you (always)
I'm here for you (forever)
Knowing good and well,
When souls sent by the stars intervene,
When predestined plans come knocking,
The temporary bond will break.
The strong hold mistaken as forever;
Cracks, unraveled, undone.
Our hands will go off on their own
To create other lives,
To touch other worlds,
To feel other hearts.
When all is said and done,
Our hands will separate.
I brace for the part
For a head start.

Older

Sasha Alex Sloan

1:03   2:33

Generational Wounds

I have issues;
You have them too
Can see right through you,
Unlike the moon

You're never shining
Always so blue
What do you need
To feel like *you*?

Is it worth it to be you?
To sell vanity and sell truth?

The Gods keep punishing those
Like you.

At least we'll get flowers when we die,
The only comfort we receive,
Staring up at the sky, raging, *why*?

**Substance Abuse and Mental Health National Helpline:*
800.662.4357

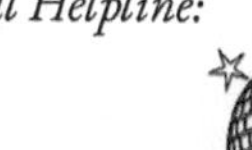

C'est Comme Ça
Paramore
0:58
1:58

Cloudburst

I want to be sunshine
I want to ignite
(But I think...)

I want to be starlight
I want to galvanize
(But I think...)

I can't be mysterious
'Cause my full time is delirium
(I'm delirious)

No point in hoping
Meaning and chaos
Are interwoven.

Can't find inner peace
Don't want what's best for me
The quiet in healing is boring

Rushes and thrills get me soaring
Yet...
All my mistakes

Keep me mourning
Keep me up
Till the morning

I want to be sunshine
My monsoons quiet
I want to be starlight

(But I think...)
No, I know
I'm a full blown downpour

I Love Me
Demi Lovato
0:12
0:57

Manic Habits

Mindfully starve all day
Eating feels like admitting to defeat
Feeding is cheating
I know I've been good
When the first sip hits
That cold glass of water
The only thing to touch my lips
The way the liquid envelopes
Fills my intestines and develops
Thanking me for so much room
The only things left in my fridge
Are cucumbers and melon juice

National Association of Anorexia Nervosa and Associated Disorders:
888.375.7767

Bigger Person
Lauren Spencer Smith
1:03
2:38

Nightmares are also Dreams

Sweetness with a little craze
Like burning sugar just for haze
The crowds were wild
Poor, beat down child
Pop the pills, go get laid

Chug the booze and light the sage
The chills, the roll
It's all so slow
Trying to conceal the pain
Connecting but still feeling insane

Smoke and mirrors, sinking games
Looking but seeing's not the same
Swipe left, swipe right
No one's in sight
Still running from your ego's shame

Like, *who the hell built my name?*
You'll never know
Need some control
Banking on your spirit's gain
Hoping one day you will change

**Substance Abuse and Mental Health National Helpline:*
800.662.4357

The Wind
Russ
0:10
5:00

Conversation with my Inner Child

I wonder often about true love and its mystical, mythical properties
I hear the secrets of nature through chattering clouds
I see the ancient world and am mesmerized by its wisdom
I want to be unforgettable, to never fade
I fear being conquered
I am enough

I pretend I am pure
I feel the moon's longing for intimacy
I touch the decadence of stars
I worry about my liberty
I weep for my essence and its inquisitive desires
I am worthy

I understand that nothing is guaranteed
I say *I will make it*
I dream of places, people yet to be discovered
I try to search for my own salvation
I hope to find my life's purpose
I am capable

Scars To Your Beautiful

Alessia Cara

1:18

1:47

To Feel Pretty

It's a constant battle
Every day
Measuring calories
The math all day
But still keep appearances
'Cause they'll always have something to say
You eat too much
Or too little
Just split me down the middle
I'll be my ideal then
Half madness, half thin
Too big
Too small
Congrats on that loss
With a smile and a wave
Oh, look at that gain
With a face of grotesque disdain
How the hell am I supposed to stay sane?
It's always, always, about my weight
It's commoner's commentary at this rate

**National Association of Anorexia Nervosa and Associated Disorders:*
888.375.7767

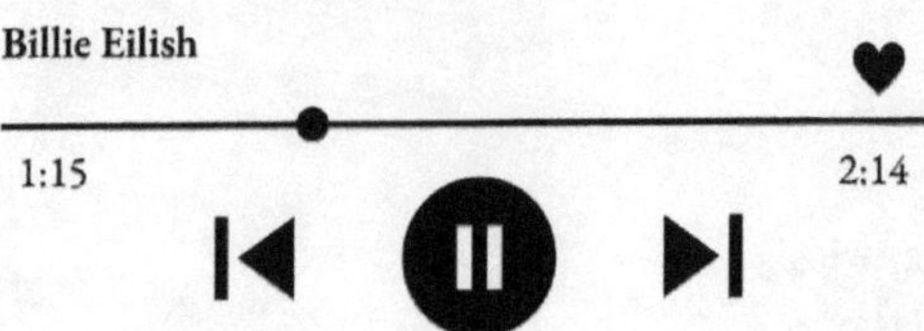
idontwannabeyouanymore
Billie Eilish
1:15
2:14

Honestly

I feel guilty for feeling hungry.
I only ever feel like a champion
When I'm famished.
When the day is gone and surpassed
And I am able to block out all the foods that harass;
The triumph,
The victory
Of looking sickly.
It's the only time
I truly ever feel pretty.
I don't care the cost,
Even if it's life lost.
I'd rather die,
Meek and thin,
Than to be forced to endure
Others' unwanted opinions
And take it on the chin.

**National Association of Anorexia Nervosa and Associated Disorders:*
888.375.7767

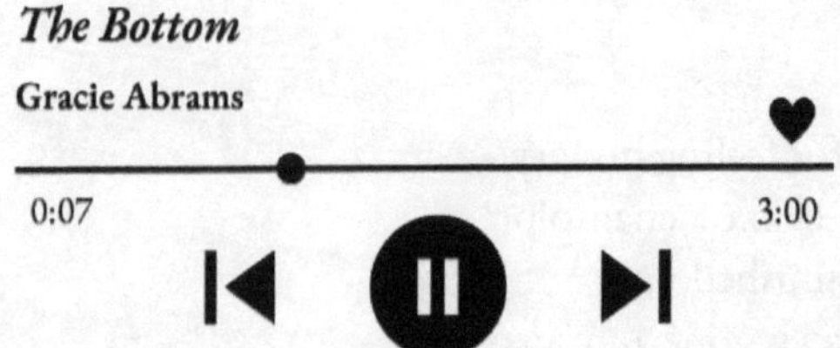
The Bottom
Gracie Abrams
0:07
3:00

I Don't Want to Date Anymore (Part I)

I hate new people.
I mean, love interests.
It's all fresh and fun
And they want a run
Down, of it all:
Who you are,
Where you're from,
Your habits and what makes you torn.
Here's the thing though,
Now, it's someone else,
Another something that gets to look past the shell,
All to put me back on the shelf.

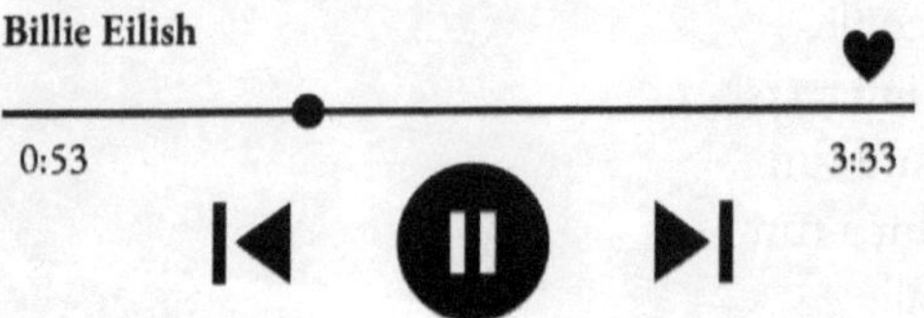

What Was I Made For? [From The Motion Picture "Barbie"]
Billie Eilish
0:53
3:33

I Don't Want to Date Anymore (Part II)

I'm a phantom of myself;
This light cost me years in the dark throws.
You're just another body to see right through
The fact that I can't look past my own.
I'm too preoccupied with how my jeans fit, okay?
Are they looser, tighter, have I retained water today?
Now, you notice; I try not to feast.
I'm almost never hungry
Until our relationship is starting to taste like defeat.
Now, you see me; I'm famished and ravish,
Bingeing and cringing.
I'd rather stay full and swallow
Than give you words that show you
Just how broken and hollow
I am.
Now, you're concerned.
Will you even be here
When my weight fluctuates
And I'm fighting body aches
From denying myself?
Scared of trans fats and nutrients,
Now I'm hooked up getting transfusions
Again...
Why do you pretend to care?
We both know you're going to run scared.

**National Association of Anorexia Nervosa and Associated Disorders:*
888.375.7767

Lately (feat. Bugus & Musa)
Russ, Bugus, Musa
1:11
1:47

Overthinker

Is the wild child of a flower child
A wild flower abloom?
Or are the flower's wiles to come into power soon?
If so, then rebels for peace
Did not die within tombs.

Is the old soul
Still an old soul
Although presently anew?
For an ancient bowl was once thought
An innovative cue;
An old soul can be new
In certain views.

Is a drifter still a drifter
If not from the sea?
Today's pictures show sails
Amongst the streets.
The new drifter begs and pleads.

With this chime, I question generations' time.
Will this rhyme flourish
Into yet another deafening mime?
Are these questions damned
To never be defined?

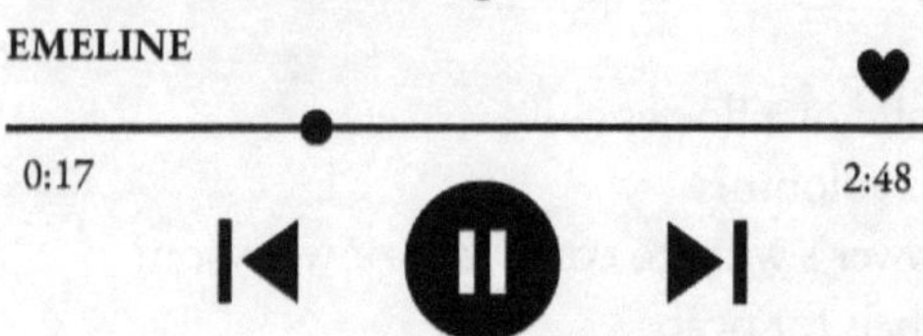

what it means to be a girl
EMELINE
0:17
2:48

Scornful Woman's Spell

Pinch of rust
Speck of dust
We're taught very young
To *endure* this kind of lust

Dash of salt
Crumb of pain
Suck the fat
Splurge on a new mane

Pick me
Choose me
Love me
I'm a product

Buy me
In that window of despair
Your fancy dressed-up derrière
Could cost you your life

If you don't hide it well
It's innocent, harmless reduction
But you still blame us for seduction
When all the fun has turned

Don't worry
No one will even bat an eye
They're all unconcerned
After all, since childhood

Silence is what we've learned

**National Sexual Assault Hotline:*
800.656.4673

When Will I Be Mine?

Hailey Orion

0:00   4:01

FUCK!!! The Patriarchy

Trust that lunar dust composed me
S.E.X. and celestial crusts engross me
Tin man with a cotton hand will betroth me
What more could a girl want?

To dethrone
He.
Watch his kingdom play
Watch the people sway
As they look the other way

Vile power hands at play
I refuse to obey
What society has pushed upon me
Our voices, we'll raise

It's hell we'll shake awake
When you come to look upon me
You won't see a slave
You can't look the other way

While this kingdom pays
You'll burn eternities
In the very flames
You woefully praise

Overthinker

INZO

0:00   4:28

Hue-Man

Daughter of di Prima's rant[1].
Surviving the war against imagination.
I wasn't dropped on my head.
This head was dropped on me.
Lugging around the material world
And the dew of its sorrows.
In an effort to heal myself,
I took to bartering with the elements.
With Water, I sold the outline of who I used to be
For my creativity between the ages of one through three.
With Fire, I negotiated for authentic vision,
Which only cost five of my fondest memories.
With Wind, I exchanged the taint of my shadow
For an aura of Northern Lights.
With Earth, I traded the flavor of heartache
For a prescription of growth and tranquility.
When communicating with each,
I discovered sacred things.
Morsels of myself reflected back to me
In others who I could be.
Mystic worlds embedded in one,
The fabric of being.
How vibrant a human can be.

---

1 Poet, Diane di Prima's poem "Rant"

Sanctuary
INZO
0:11
3:22

Simplicity

Simplicity,
That is what's calling me.
Nature's longevity,
Watching so stealthily.

Simplicity,
That is who calls to me.
Minimal tendencies,
Saving serenity.

Simplicity,
Silent sweet reverie.
Blending eternities,
Losing all gravity.

Simplicity,
Wholesome remedy.

Originally published in Merak Magazine

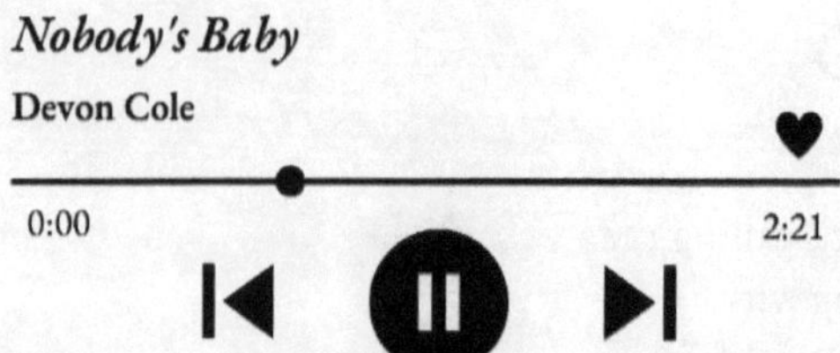

Nobody's Baby
Devon Cole
0:00
2:21

Holy, Never Lonely

What are your values?
I have all but two.

Autonomy & courage.

Yes, that is it.
Autonomy & courage.

If you happen to share these values,
The masses might venture to proclaim that I am the girl for you.

Although... truthfully, I hope it's the latter.
Not because I find you lacking,

But rather,
Because I do not wish to be the girl for you.

I do not wish to be the *woman* for you.
I wish
To be
Nothing

To anyone.
I solely wish to be
Me.

Entirely, completely
Me.

Alone.
In the best company.

Fulfilled, genuinely content.
Enthralled
By myself.

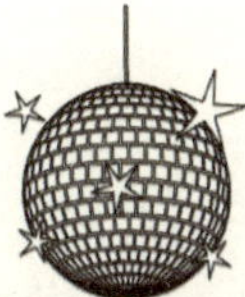

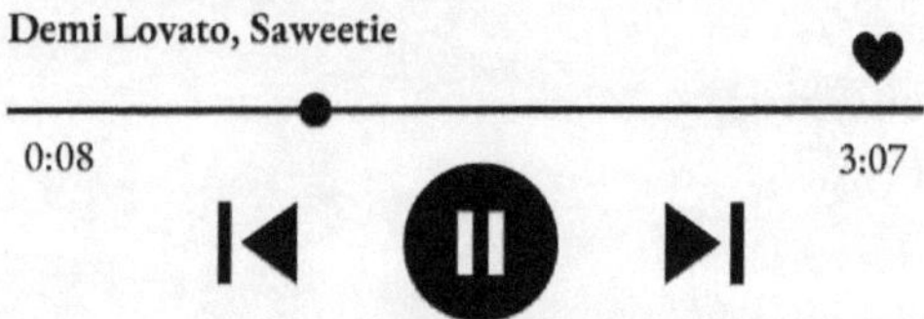

My Girlfriends Are My Boyfriend (feat. Saweetie)
Demi Lovato, Saweetie
0:08
3:07

Unconditional Love

Everything I've ever learned of love,
Authentic, genuine, real, true love,
Has been from my sisters.
Never has love revealed itself to me
Romantic.
Never has love ever revealed itself
Familial.

I have learned of love
From love.
All that love has taught me
Has been demonstrated by the family that *chose* me.
I, in return,
They.
I *chose* them.

No conditions, logic, or reason.
Zero judgment,
Regardless of season.
We *chose* each other.
To show up for each other
And continue
To *choose*
To *love*.

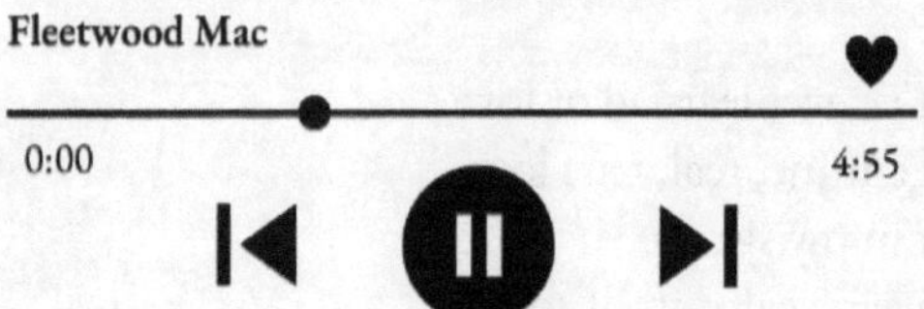

Gold Dust Woman - 2004 Remaster
Fleetwood Mac
0:00
4:55

Psyche Before Cupid

Thunder woman
Lightning smile
Herb child

Elysian muse
Lotus-eater
Storm Earth Flame

Speak in spells
Move like rain
Potions in her veins

Every motion
Guided by willow
Dances like a sage

Walks like rhythm
Sinks in planes
Wicked ways

Wild honey
Bletting dew
Kalon lips

Bid adieu

Rhiannon

Fleetwood Mac

0:00   4:12

Daughter of the Moon

Luscious red curls
Illustrious cherry pearls
With constellations in her eyes
She brews hypnosis at midnight

Baptized in her name
Here nothing can be tame
Just between us
This world's not enough

From cyclones, she benefits
The moon, her catalyst
Solar affair's child
With eclectic vials

Evergreen staples and cobblestone walls
Cast iron cauldrons as rain patter lulls
The burn of the flame forever engulfs
Hell's bells and love spells

With pragmatic, fragrant fairy floss
Strawberry Sundays
Violet-kissed Mondays
Married in the way

The stars are to the night sky
Through and by, the universe
Unto the end of times
And therefore

Here after
Ever thine,
Ever by
Lunar dye

Daughter of a King

Trailer Flowers

0:00   1:34

I am Enough

Father, oh father,
Who doesn't leave behind,
You've taught me to love darkness,
Sublime and divine.
Subliminal and criminal,
How can you be so kind?
I've looked into your eyes
And see the way I shine.
My shadow isn't lack of light.
Your presence is near,
Forgiving and beginning.
Protective father of mine,
I thank you for your mercy
Your grace and your time.

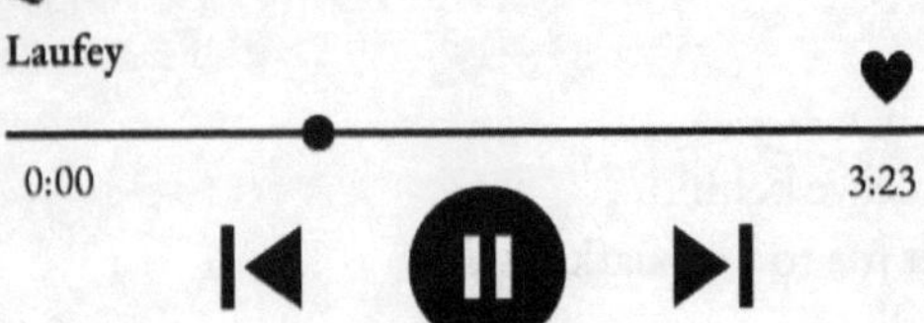

Questions For The Universe
Laufey
0:00
3:23

Violets & Rye

Blue lotus tightly packed into sacred texts
The satisfying crackle of a
Steady psalm's smooth burn
Sacrosanct smoke, pucker punch toke
Staring at a bowl-shaped moon
Darkness has spilled out across the sky
And here I sit
Smoking scriptures
Writing my own
Sipping on smoldered rye
Defining home

Thank you for choosing my universe.

It Was Always You

Daisy Jones

0:00   1:46

From the Vault

Play *It Was Always You* by Daisy Jones

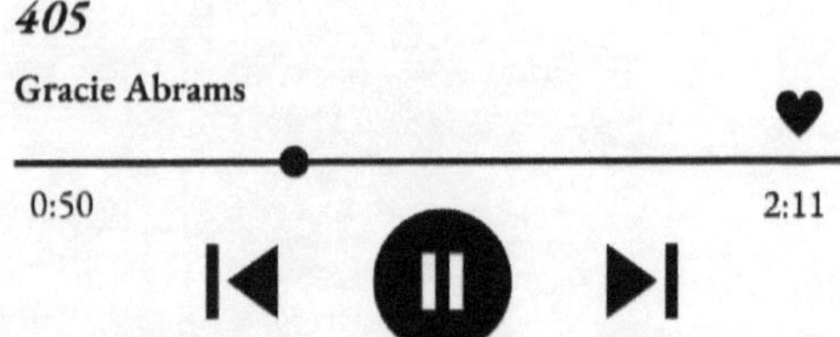
405
Gracie Abrams
0:50
2:11

Promise
Laufey
0:14
2:10

Please Redeem (Part I)

Lukewarm highs,
Why couldn't you do me the kindness?
Why didn't you lie?

My frozen heart,
You daggered and bruised.
Committing
Three consistent dates;
She must've been first rate.

Persistent echoes,
Relentless reams.
The pit,
My mind,
Resounding screams.

STILL C U

Jessie Reyez

0:58   2:19

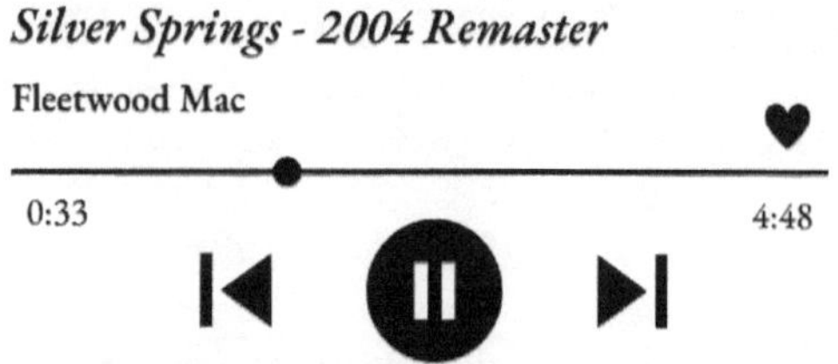

Silver Springs - 2004 Remaster

Fleetwood Mac

0:33   4:48

Please Redeem (Part II)

My old space;
Her new place.
What kind of sick twisted crime?
I'm not healed,
Not one bit
By time.

Under your sheets?
Clever.
Under my skin?
Never.
It's not the girl you fucked,
It's the one that got you cucked.

Skin crawls,
Heart thaws.
"I'm not the one for him"
Must my thoughts be this grim?
She'll get your hymns.
You only ever saw me as sin.

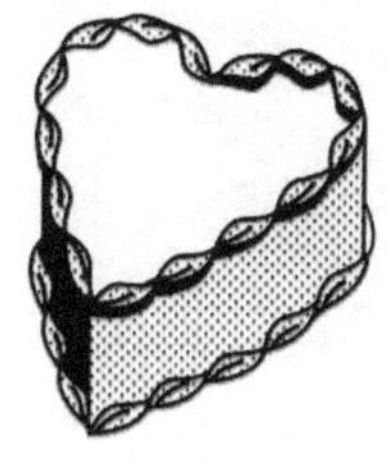

Choose To Choose Me

Notes & Acknowledgments

*All of the songs mentioned in *Choose To Choose Me* are copyrighted to the individual artist(s) of each song. Thank you for acting as the soundtrack to my collection of organized chaos.

It's said that it takes a village to raise a child, and I have never known something to be more true. This work is a piece of me, birthed by me; through failures and successes. *Choose To Choose Me* is my baby and this baby could not have made it here, to these printed pages, into your special hands, without my village.

Angela, if it wasn't for you pushing and hounding me about the world needing my words, this book would never exist.

To my gorgeous girls, Camber, Carly, Katherine, Katya, Mia, and Vanessa—in each of you is the woman I strive to be. I would not be here without the endless support, compassion, and love that you literal goddesses so freely and consistently extend to me.

To my publisher, editor, confidant, and sometimes part-time therapist—Flor Ana and Indie Earth Publishing, thank you for your patience and always being down to go on this crazy ride with me.

To my favorite person in the whole world, Aidan, through your eyes I've learned to see myself and the world in a much softer light than I ever thought I could. Thank you for being my heart, my motivation, and my number one fan always. I love you so much, little bear.

To one specific muse, thank you for seeing so much beauty, value, and honor in me when I couldn't quite see it yet in myself, for myself. I learned so much from each of my muses, but for you, I am eternally grateful. The moments we shared, every single one of our experiences, they all shaped me into the woman I am today.

Thank you to the creatives who helped me make my vision for the cover of this book come true. From making and designing the cake to all the hard work of angles, careful shadows and silhouettes when photographing, your artistic eyes and talented hands are gifts to humanity.

Thank you to my advanced readers and generous authors who gifted me their time and brilliant words. Your interactions with my chaotic scriptures are a precious treasure that I will cherish and hold onto dearly forever.

And of course, to my readers—*that's insane to think about. I have readers.* I am continuously humbled and honored by your voluntary investment in sharing this experience with me. Embarking on this journey with me and *choosing* me. I will never be able to thoroughly articulate how much our connection means to me. I hope to somehow carry a little piece of you within me as a little piece of this book lives on within each of you. In *choosing* me, dear reader, you allowed me to *choose* you.

About the Author

© Carl-Frederick Francois

Elizabeth Knightly is a passionate writer and poet, exploring themes of love, loss and self-discovery in her evocative verses. She values truth, authenticity and transparency above all else and wants her readers to find morsels of themselves in her words. When Elizabeth is not writing, she is tasting different perspectives and experiences through her solo-travel adventures and time-traveling to appreciate all things vintage, including black and white films, Audrey Hepburn, and cars that look straight out of *The Great Gatsby*. Nothing makes her feel more alive than Taylor Swift and the way lightning crackles across an inky raven sky. To Liz, rainy days feel like sunshine.

Connect with Elizabeth
Instagram: @lizknightlywrites

About the Publisher

Indie Earth Publishing is an independent, author-first co-publishing company based in Miami, FL, dedicated to giving authors and writers the creative freedom they deserve when it comes to publishing their works. Indie Earth combines the freedom of self-publishing with the support and backing of traditional publishing for poetry, fiction, short story collections, and children's books by providing a plethora of services meant to aid them in the book publishing experience. A publisher for writers founded by a writer, with Indie Earth Publishing, you are more than just another author, you are part of the Indie Earth creative community, making a difference one book at a time.

www.indieearthbooks.com

Instagram: @indieearthbooks

For inquiries, please email:
indieearthbooks@gmail.com